I0159413

1

ABC of Astrology

by

Bernie Morris

Published by Bronwyn Editions in the United Kingdom
2010

Cover design by Linda Koperski © 2009

Internal vignettes by Bernie Morris & Linda Koperski

Printed by Lightning Source UK 2010

Other titles by Bronwyn Editions:

'Bobby's Girl' 2009 by Bernie Morris

'Kids We Were' 2008 by Bernie Morris

'An A-Z of Looney Limericks' 2009 by Bernie Morris
and Linda Koperski

'Verse for Ages' 2009 by Colleen Thatcher
and Bernie Morris

One Brit, One Bike and One BIG Country 2010
by John McKay

Bronwyn Editions: www.bronwynwrite.vpweb.co.uk

Acknowledgements

To:

Linda, my super cover artist, who is now launching a new career for herself in graphic design. Bronwyn will miss you.

Bob and Koi who will be taking over from Linda in the cover design department.

Carole Devine, my American friend and Astrologer, who has been so supportive and has contributed the foreword.

Everyone who has ever been mildly intrigued by Astrology. Remember that the following chapters do not constitute any personal horoscopes. They are simply a list of general attributes of each sign, just for your interest.

If you do indeed want a personal horoscope, you need to contact a professional Astrologer, such as Carole: www.devineadvantage.com

Foreword

Surely there must be thousands of books and articles describing the Sun Signs, but seldom have I seen one that is so much fun, so accurate, and so easy to digest as this unique collection of wise observations.

Bernie Morris has analyzed each sign and attributed one trait to each of the letters of the alphabet for all of them. In her usual down-to-earth style, she reveals her sensitive understanding of the human persona in all its myriad manifestations. In all her books, she has demonstrated her ability to peel away the projections we all use to protect ourselves, and expose the core archetype seeking expression beneath—even though her other books are not necessarily about astrology.

We all learn best when material is presented in an entertaining way. Don't let the simplicity of this presentation mislead you! You may have received this book as a light-hearted gift, or picked it up as an entertaining distraction. But, in the end, you'll be amazed at how much more you understand your spouse, mother or son. Doesn't it make life much more fulfilling when we are able to see the "why" behind our companions' behaviour? You'll turn to this book over and over to remind yourself of all the possible nuances of behaviour you are encountering in new acquaintances, as well as familiar ones. Social interaction becomes easier; negotiations go better; and life, in general, is smoother when we *really* understand the basic needs and personality traits of those around us.

And the best part is that it is short, pithy and gets to the point in language anyone can understand. In this busy world, it is exactly what we need.

Carole Devine
www.devineadvantage.com
December 28, 2009

ARIES

Aries

Aries is the forward type
He doesn't lose his head
Except when rushing headlong in
Where angels fear to tread

ABC of ARIES

Assertion – Aries is the sign of progression and assertion. You will therefore always make your presence felt in one way or another, no matter what the circumstances. Aries has tremendous drive and little patience. He or she would like everything done yesterday.

Bold – Brimming with confidence, you were born to strut your stuff and to lead the way forward. You have no qualms about risk-taking either. As an innate adventurer, you probably enjoy the sense of excitement and danger.

Crusader – Yes, you can be quite heroic. You are the first to take up a good cause for others, and to fight magnificently on behalf of your compatriots or colleagues. People may look to you to solve their grievances, and some of these may cause you a few headaches – yet you cannot resist a challenge in any shape or form; you will accept them all ungrudgingly.

Diamond – The precious stone which is most associated with Aries. Its hardness and brightness are unequalled in nature. You should definitely try to own at least one of these delightful gems – preferably several.

Enterprise – Ruled by the planet Mars, you naturally know how to get the stuff you want. Energy, dynamism, and innovation are your toys to play with. But try not to tread on too many toes along the way, else you could leave a trail of resentment in your wake.

Fearless – This is what you naturally are: a pioneer; an adventurer. You have never crossed swords with that strange little thing called 'fear'. Just remember – there are eleven other zodiac types out there, all with different tricks up their sleeves. You would be well-advised not to become too complacent.

Generous – Yes, you are generous to a fault, especially towards lovers and friends. You will give without counting the cost. Only beware of those who would take advantage of your generosity.

Head – The body part which is most associated with Aries, down as far as the eyes. You will either be prone to severe headaches, or you will never get them, even when you most deserve to. Your hair may sport a reddish tinge, regardless of overall colour. This may quickly recede from the forehead in males. Eyes may be light-coloured with a steely gaze.

Of course you are innately headstrong – so carry on and do whatever you must, so long as it is socially acceptable.

Iron – The base metal most strongly associated with this sign. These days, there are many modern forms: steel; stainless steel; chrome, etc. Even rusted iron: red ferrous oxide, has some good uses for gardeners. You will probably have many items made of this bright metal in your home (especially knives or tools). You are likely to have an iron will to match.

Jeopardy – The dictionary says this means risk of loss, harm or death. But an Aries will pay no mind to such warnings. To him or her, 'risk' means challenge or adventure and he/she will embrace it with open arms

Kinetic – Being highly energetic, you can probably not bear to keep still for a moment, and will suffer agonies in any enforced situation of this kind. Although a very physical sign, you will find this kind of restraint more easily bearable if your mind is thoroughly occupied.

Love at First Sight – No other sign can fall in love so instantly and so fatally. You might be down on your knees, offering the sun, moon and stars to your loved one, and rejection will be very hard for you to accept. On the other hand, your love can 'switch off' just as instantly if a new conquest is sighted. You will need to think very hard about what you really want – forever.

Mars – The ruler of Aries (called Ares in Greek mythology). Mars is traditionally associated with war, blood, fire, sexuality, cruelty, and all things masculine. These days, astrologers know better – we know that those are the extremely negative traits of Mars. The positive ones are those to be cultivated and utilised, for everyone has the planet Mars in their chart somewhere – yet not everyone is Attila the Hun.

The positive aspects of Mars are: energy; enterprise; progression and achievement. These are the helpful ways in which you should use your powerful ruler.

Novel – Yes, you like anything new and modern, and are probably the first to upgrade or update your possessions, whilst quickly discarding anything outworn or dated. You are quite innovative in your own right, probably full of ideas for inventions and improvements. So why not give them a whirl?

Outspoken – An Arien hardly ever stops to think before speaking, so you may therefore open your mouth and put your foot in it fairly often. Of course you want to speak your mind – at least you are telling the truth as you see it, and at least everyone knows where they stand with you. Diplomacy will never be on your list of finer talents, however.

Pioneering – Being a natural pioneer, Aries likes to be first, a groundbreaker, or even record-breaker. That is why so many of you are sportsmen or speedsters.

Although it is not easy these days to be the forerunner of anything – as so much has already been achieved – you should still enjoy the challenge of doing your utmost.

Quick-thinking – No other sign has such lightning thought processes or faster reactions. Some of you can probably compute in your head quicker than others can press buttons on a calculator, and you don't have much patience with slower-witted people either. In fact, you hate waiting for anything; so probably don't have much patience at all.

Red – This is the colour most strongly associated with Aries: the colour of its ruling planet Mars. Various shades of orange and burgundy are also acceptable, as well as bright bold pinks, often favoured by Arien females; for all of these are mutations of the basic 'red'.

This colour preference is often unconsciously extended to favourite foods and drink. For example: most Ariens have a liking for red meat and hot spicy dishes, such as, chilli-con-carne. Other red foods, such as, tomatoes, strawberries, salmon, or beetroot may also be liked. And red wine is sure to be a winner.

Straightforward – Yes, you are direct and forthright – no beating around the bush for you! The upside of this is that you are scrupulously honest and probably don't have a devious bone in your body. With you, what folks see is what they get.

The downside could be: that you sometimes upset people by saying exactly what you think. The acquisition of sensitivity could become a valuable notch to your bow.

Temper – Many of you are likely to have a 'short fuse', that is a quick and furious temper. You could try 'counting to ten', as they say, but it probably wouldn't work. Fortunately, this usually blows over very quickly, and you may find yourself wondering what you were mad about.

You are not one to hold grudges either, as you tend to 'forgive and forget' just as fast as you do everything else.

Undaunted – You are not one to learn by experience and your mistakes because, for you, each moment in time is a brand-new experience, and mistakes are things you will never admit to. And so you will sail through life, gleefully "rushing in where angels fear to tread" and probably getting away with it – that's the amazing thing.

Vulcan – The Roman god of fire and metalwork: an excellent patron for Aries. In mythology, he was a heavenly blacksmith, and actually forged the weapons for Mars (the god of War) to use in battle.
   But if you are more inclined to associate the word "Vulcan" with *Star Trek*, that's OK too. These logical, straightforward and honest people, who have overcome their primitive past in favour of progression and achievement, are the very epitome of all the positive qualities of Aries.

Winner – You were born to be: you will be; you must be, or you will spend your life trying to be. You have a greater incentive than most people – so don't let *me* hold you up. Get on and do it!

Xenophanes – A Greek philosopher: a critic of the belief that the gods resembled human beings. He was a proponent of a form of monotheism, arguing that there is a single, eternal, self-sufficient Consciousness which influences the universe.
   He was most likely an Arien.

Yang – In Chinese philosophy, the male or active principle of the two opposing forces of the universe, the opposite force being YIN (female/receptive).

The typical Arien probably needs a bit of YIN in order to achieve his/her own balance and harmony.

Zealous – There is not much more to be said about the keenness, eagerness, and zest for life of an Aries.

Just live it as you were born to.

Strike while the iron is hot

TAURUS

Taurus

Taurus has a pretty face
And likes her comfort best
She'll eat you out of house and home
Then take the longest rest

ABC of Taurus

ART – Taurus is an Earth sign and therefore quite worldly, yet probably appreciates beauty and art more than any other. Many of you will have artistic or musical talent yourselves, and this sign is often blessed with a deep and melodious singing voice. Even if this should not be the case, you should still enjoy building a fine collection of your favourite pieces.

BUILDER – From your earliest days on the beach, you would have been happily building sandcastles, dams and bridges, perhaps becoming quite upset when the sea washed away your creations. The desire to build is deeply-rooted in Taurus. Many of you end up as civil engineers, archaeologists, or owning vast empires of chain stores.

Although not naturally a destructive sign, you may find frustration difficult to take and – in a rare storm of temper, could actually destroy your own creation, then deeply regret it afterwards.

COPPER – The metal which is most strongly associated with your Venus ruler and therefore with Taurus. Green in its natural state; when burnished acquires the most unique and delicate colour of brownish-rose – impossible to put a name to, other than "copper". Widely used in the building trade, especially in electric wiring and plumbing.

Traces can also be absorbed through the human skin when worn as jewellery, thus giving its mineral value. Copper also has many ornamental and decorative uses – all pleasing to the Taurean eye.

DOMESTICITY – In the sense of being Lord or Lady of the Manor, your home is the place you most like to rule. Beauty and comfort will be your prime considerations therein. This is where you will "put your feet up", feed your face with all your favourite food, and watch whatever you like on TV. You will take no advice or interference on how to run your home, for this is your domain – your castle. You should also enjoy entertaining rather than visiting because, as host or hostess, you will be entirely in control of the show, which is sure to be a magnificent feast.

ENDURING – When times are at their very worst, Taurus can "weather the storms" the very best. This is where the strength and endurance of "the Bull" really comes into its own. No other Sign can stand its ground so firmly, nor take as much punishment as this one.

So, if a friend needs moral support in a crisis – they should definitely choose you!

FOOD – Obviously important to everyone as one of Life's essentials, but perhaps especially so to Taurus. Food is far more than the mainstay of your existence. To you it is a great luxury to be enjoyed. You will appreciate the finest and the best, and the most expensive that you can afford will grace your table. You are most likely an excellent cook – if not, you will make sure that your partner or spouse is.

The way to your heart is surely through your stomach.

GREEN-FINGERED – Even if you have never tried gardening, you will probably find that this is true, for Taurus is so "in touch" with the earth and creative ability, that you would be most unlikely to fail.

Growing prize flowers would enhance your artistic sense and natural pride. Whereas growing organic vegetables would greatly satisfy your innate need to "provide". Taurus has also an affinity with trees. Try apple, as one of the most rewarding and versatile of fruits. And, after pruning, apple-wood will smell gorgeous on your log fire or barbecue.

HANDSOME – Ruled by Venus, Taurus is often blessed with the finest looks in the Zodiac. Men are handsome – women are beautiful. Perfect heart-shaped faces are common, and men may be tempted to grow beards or adopt weird hairstyles in order to look more macho and rugged. Eyes in particular are usually large, limpid, and curly-lashed (like the Bull), often with a serene gaze which can be soothing to others. These same eyes, however, can flash with unexpected fury during those rare explosions of Taurean temper (the Bull in a china shop).

These fits of rage can be quite alarming to others, as they seem so out of character. Fortunately, they only occur when you have reached the end of your tether, which is a long one.

INDULGENT – To others as well as to yourself. With a sign that is so appreciative of all the finest things Earth has to offer, this trait is not very surprising.

You will love to give, especially from your own territory, so you may prefer to entertain from home rather than visit others for entertainment. Any parties you give will be sure to be extravagant.

Venus, the goddess of beauty, richness and bounty, will always be with you.

JADE – I have chosen this stone first for Taurus, not alone for its beautiful shade of pale green, but also because it is more mineral than gemstone, and therefore more "earthy". It is also more widely-used than other jewels for ornamental or artistic design. Emerald or peridot would also be acceptable to Taurus.

You should definitely try to own or wear at least one of these precious stones.

KNIGHT – Just like the knights of old, you are chivalrous, valiant, protective, stalwart, and a champion of your beliefs. Maybe you would not lead the charge, like an Aries, but you would definitely run the longest distance. Your staying power is more suited to "Quest" than "Confrontation".

LAID-BACK – This expression could be taken quite literally in your case, for you do not simply "sit in a chair", you collapse and sprawl into it and, if it is a reclining chair, you recline. Why not? That's what chairs are for: relaxing.

Generally speaking though, yours is the calmest and most serene approach to Life. You are not prone to stress, and will idly watch with mild amusement as others get into a state about nothing much – then extend a helpful hoof.

It takes an awful lot for you to see the "red rag" – an awful, awful lot.

MATERIALISTIC – As the "middle" Earth sign, you are quite naturally materialistic. Heaven is "right down here" for you. You probably don't have much faith in Fairies, Angels, Religion, or anything mystical or unworldly. The "here and now" suits you just fine.

Of course, you will need money and possessions to achieve your "heaven on earth" – there is no other way to your heart's desire. And so you will spend your life in the acquisition of a sublime lifestyle. This will be your main driving force.

NOSE – This is the body part, along with ears and throat, which is most associated with Taurus. In childhood, you may have been prone to infections of these areas, and still you should take the utmost care of them, for at least three of your five senses are involved here.

Aromatherapy is something you might find pleasant and beneficial.

OPINIONATED – You believe what you believe, regardless of any influence or arguments from others. As if carved in stone, you are virtually immovable in your opinions.

POSSESSIVE – Yes, you are possessive about all that is rightfully yours, and might also want to be about much which is not. You could easily become covetous or avaricious.

The upside of this tendency is the love and care which you will lavish upon your family, friends, and possessions alike. You will place the utmost value on all of these things, and will never a waster be.

QUANTITY – And quality. As a Taurean, you naturally want the most and the best, and you are quite willing to pay up front for such acquisition. The danger here is that if you obtain too much at too early a stage in your life, there will be nothing much left for you to work towards, and you could become stagnant, lazy, or dispirited.

REALISTIC – This being something you have in common with the other two Earth signs (Capricorn and Virgo). You are all "down-to-earth" and realistic. But perhaps because you, Taurus, are middle earth, you are less inclined to be influenced by others, and so will invariably "see the wood" as well as the trees.

You are certainly more of a gnome than a pixie.

STUBBORN – Of all the signs in the zodiac, you definitely take the rosette here. Obstinate, willful, pig-headed, mulish, adamant, uncompromising, and unyielding are words which immediately spring to mind. You have your feet firmly planted in the earth and you like it fine just where you are, thank you very much!

The upside of this, of course, is that you will "stick to your guns" no matter what the opposition may say.

You will never a turncoat be.

TERRITORIAL – Taurus very much needs his/her own space, whether in private or public life, and will positively resent any intrusion or encroachment upon this. At work, you would like your own office or department or, at least, your own desk and phone. At home, you probably have your own favourite chair, coffee mug or beer glass.

On a much larger scale, you would like to own or manage property or land, if you don't already.

Yes, you were born to be Master or Mistress of all you behold.

UP – This is the only direction you will ever be prepared to take. So don't look down on the way.

VENUS – The Planet which rules Taurus. Often visible as a bright star in the eastern sky just before sunrise, when it is known as the Morning Star. Personified as the Roman goddess of beauty, love and bounty.

WEALTH – If Venus is well-placed in your Natal Chart, then it is unlikely that you will ever want for anything in the material sense. Wealth and affluence should come to you naturally. Other forms of wealth could include: good looks; charm; peace; harmony; and many friends.

X – In mathematics, "X" = multiplication.

YEOMEN – Very much a British association (sorry, but 'Y's a difficult one). The Yeomen of the Guard were instigated in Tudor times as personal bodyguards to the

27

King or Queen. One was usually elected to taste the Monarch's meals before serving, to ensure the food had not been poisoned – hence the name: Beefeater (how very Taurean).

Beefeaters are no longer expected to carry out this irksome duty, but can still be seen today, wearing the same bright snazzy uniform, all padded out to make them look beefy and bulky.

ZEUS – King of the gods in ancient Greece (Jupiter in Rome). Zeus was fairly benign most of the time, looking down with mild amusement at the antics of us mortals. But woe betide you if you angered him, for then he would rise from his throne and cast down thunderbolts which shook the very earth (just like a Taurean). He even adopted the guise of a bull once or twice, so he must have been sympathetic to Taurus.

Home is where the heart is

GEMINI

Gemini

Gemini's the coolest guy
With the very latest view
He quickly loses interest though
And moves to pastures new

ABC of Gemini

AGILE – Gemini is the most active sign next to Aries; but rather than moving forward in a direct fashion, Gemini tends to dart around, constantly changing direction. Agile of mind as well as body, this sign needs constant mental stimulation, else will become easily bored.

BRAINY – Being ruled by Mercury, the planet of intellect, you are almost bound to be highly intelligent. Trying to spread yourself too thinly could become a problem though. The trouble is: you want to know everything there is to know and will therefore try to cram too much, too fast into your memory. It is simply not possible to know everything there is to know within the human lifespan.

You should try to give your brain a rest sometimes.

COMMUNICATIVE – Most Gemini's love to talk – especially to discuss and debate. But even if you are not a great conversationalist, you should enjoy writing letters, e-mails, or just plain writing.

You may consider the telephone to be the best invention ever.

DEXTROUS – The hands are the body part most associated with Gemini, as well as the arms, shoulders, chest and lungs but, most noticeably, the hands. Geminian hands are usually finely-shaped and expressive with great dexterity and speed. For this reason, Gemini's are often adept musicians, cartoonists, or typists.

Anything which demands speed, accuracy, and dexterity is best approached by a Gemini.

EXCITABLE – Sometimes it is difficult for you to remain calm and relaxed – you just don't have time for that! You will greet every new and interesting challenge with ebullience and glee.

Well bully for you!

FLIGHTY – Although an affectionate and friendly enough sign, Gemini mostly prefers to keep relationships on a light-hearted level, and may shy away from any deep lasting commitment. You will probably "play the field" when young and perhaps gain a reputation for flirtatiousness. Even after finally settling down, a Gemini may soon substitute romance for humour and wit, and expect a partner to be communicative, companionable and lively.

Try any other 'air' sign for your best compatibility (Aquarius or Libra), or even Sagittarius, your opposite, as this has been proved to sometimes work.

GESTICULATIVE – Your hands have a language all of their own. Whenever you speak or explain anything, they will move wildly, almost of their own accord, enhancing and demonstrating everything you say, without you even being aware of their antics. You will be good at signing, even before you ever realise it.

This is one of the true "signatures" of Gemini.

HYPERACTIVE – No other sign can expend such vast amounts of energy in so many different ways. Yet you may lack staying power if a task becomes too lengthy or tedious. A Gemini works best in short bursts; but quickly feels the need for a change and to tackle something different.

You may therefore find yourself with several projects underway at any one time, all in various stages of completion – and this is probably just the way you like it.

INDEPENDENT – You are the mutable (flexible) air sign; therefore not too worried about the need to rely on others, or what they think of you. Sure, you like people if they like you – if not, you can take them or leave them. You are definitely the best sign for 'doing your own thing'.

JACK-of-all-TRADES – With so many possible avenues open to multi-talented Gemini, you may find a choice of career rather difficult. You may actually try several different ones, just to make sure you don't miss out on anything you *could* have done. Take care that you don't spend your entire life doing this – although if you were happy and fulfilled that way, it would not really matter.

Generally speaking, Gemini likes to use the mind as well as the hands, so careers which involve both would definitely suit you best.

KNOWLEDGEABLE – Up to a point. You know a helluva lot about many different things – you have made it your business to do so. But remember, no-one lives long enough to know everything there is to know; that is just humanly impossible and an unfortunate fact of life. You have the ability to sound very knowledgeable, even if you don't know the subject very well – you can usually bluff your way through.

Make it your business to learn as much as you possibly can throughout your life.

LUNGS – These, along with the airways, may be either quite vulnerable, or powerfully efficient. You will soon find out which. If the latter, then you could be a marathon runner, athlete, play a wind instrument, or have a strong singing voice.

If the former, you should avoid all types of air pollution, if possible, live in a healthy environment, and try to avoid smoking, coal-mining, or paint-spraying.

These essential organs could be your making, or your undoing.

MERCURY – The planet which rules Gemini. Mercury is the planet of intellect and communication. In Roman mythology, the youthful messenger of the gods (Hermes in Greek).

Mercury flitted about between Heaven and Earth, with wings on his heels. He was a sort-of intercom angel.

Mercury also refers to the liquid metal which is associated with Gemini – widely used in thermometers because of its free-running properties, and also known as "quicksilver".

NEOPHILIA – Your love of anything new, and change for the sake of change, may extend to language; in which case you could become a neologist. Not only will you invent your own words and coin new phrases (like Shakespeare), you might also reinvent existing ones, and should definitely keep up with modern terminology and slang.

You could probably write a farce or spoof of anything.

OUTGOING – Your confidence stems from the fact that you don't particularly care what anyone else thinks – you are just "you" whether they like it or not.

Your popularity proves that this attitude can work.

PLAYFUL – Like a child, you sometimes don't know when "enough is enough" and this may irritate some of the more serious types. However, your playful charm and whimsical ways should definitely win most hearts.

You will always be a joker. Take care to sometimes consider when some sensitivity is appropriate.

QUIP – Yes, you are probably master of the witticism, or quick repartit. You have an ever-ready sense of humour and can also be sarcastic without seeming unkind.

RESOURCEFUL – Probably even more so than your next-door sign: Cancer. You have umpteen talents at your disposal, and any number of these can be used to extricate you from any amount of fixes.

Be sure to use your resources well.

SLIM – A typical Gemini is often slender or wiry in build. This is mainly due to the fast and frantic pace of your lifestyle – you simply don't have time to put on weight.

If you are untypical, this is probably due to your Ascendant sign, or some other influence in your chart, so see your astrologer for guidance.

TEACH – Gemini's love to impart their knowledge, and therefore make very good teachers, especially to willing pupils. You might prefer to teach very young, or mature students – those who really *want* to know.

Unfortunately, these days, children of between ages are the most difficult to reach, but – if anyone can do it, you can!

UNSYMPATHETIC – You don't mean to be – you just wish that everyone was as tough and resilient as you are.

You have no time for malingerers or skivers.

VERSATILE – THE most versatile sign of the Zodiac. You will never be short of an idea, an answer – or an escape hatch.

Always remember to use your resources well.

WILEY – You can be cunning, crafty, or devious, but this is usually in the context of practical joking – never intended to be malicious.

XANTHENE DYE – A particularly fluorescent type of yellow dye, almost dazzling to the eye, often used for marker pens or "safety" clothing. It suitably combines the flamboyant nature of Gemini with its affinitive colour: YELLOW.

YELLOW – This is the primary colour most associated with Gemini (along with other bright colours). It has nothing to do with the slang term meaning "cowardice". Yellow is the most mellow of colours, reflecting the brightness and clarity of the sun. Wearing this colour raises self-esteem and a sense of well-being. It's said that it also attracts money to the wearer (as well as bees).

ZIGZAG – This effectively describes the way in which a Gemini lives his/her life. Imagine a zigzag which is not vertical, but lying horizontally along a path.

You will most definitely progress, but with constant deviations along the way.

Many hands make light work

CANCER

Cancer

Cancer is the guardian type
A bit like Mother Hen
She'll keep you safe beneath her wing
But you might not fly again

ABC of Cancer

ARMOUR – The 'Cancerian shell' refers to the stoic suit of armour which all Cancerians wear. This armour can take many forms. It may be a veneer of reserve, humour, aloofness, or even hostility; but it always exists. Cancer is a sign which does not willingly show its true colours, except to those nearest and dearest, or closest. This sign is a bit like the proverbial iceberg: nine-tenths of the true personality is submerged, at least until he/she trusts you to know him/herself intimately.

BARGAIN – No-one appreciates a bargain more than a Cancerian. For this reason, you may often frequent car-boot sales, garage sales, rummage sales, or charity shops. Antique road shows, auctions, or free newspaper ads may also grab your attention.

You have a unique quality of being able to manage your money well. Be sure to use this to your advantage.

CREATIVE – There are few signs more creative than a Cancerian. Whether it be arts and crafts, cookery, photography, or simply making jam, you are sure to excel in any of your creative endeavours.

DEFENSIVE – Especially on behalf of those weaker than yourself. The Cancerian parent would die to defend their young, or almost die to defend their friends – be they human or animal. You may be particularly prone to lash out at those who attack you and yours. This: 'The Claw', is an innate Cancerian preservation instinct.

EMOTIONS - With the moon ruling your sign, you are practically driven by these. Do not be deterred by this idea. Emotions are very powerful influences which have spurred mankind on to the greatest of achievements.

FINANCE - Because security is so important to this sign, Cancerians are often found in jobs which deal with finance: accounts, insurance, pensions, mortgages, banks, etc. This is not to say that you are mad about money or over-materialistic, though you have good ability to save and invest, especially with loved ones in mind, and this part of your nature may be further enhanced or assisted by your imaginative and creative side.

GUARDIAN - Even if you are not a foster-parent, adoptive parent, caretaker, janitor, or guard outside Buckingham Palace, this 'guardian' trait will be evident in your personality. You are the true 'friend in need' whom everyone can trust: the ideal 'agony aunt/uncle'. Your guarding instinct can only be outweighed by your sympathy, and you are probably the world's best keeper of secrets.

HISTORY - Most Cancerians are interested in this subject; some even fascinated or 'wowed' by it. Old buildings, archives, archaeological digs, or museums are often favourite haunts, and this is one of the most likely signs to research his/her family tree. Generally speaking, anything old, ancient, or simply antique will appeal.

INTUITIVE – All water signs have the gift of intuition, and as the Cardinal one, Cancer is probably the most original of this group. You should therefore have hunches and 'gut feelings' that often turn out to be true. You should never ignore your basic instincts, as they are most probably the correct ones.

JACKDAW – This canny bird: comical, ungainly, but remarkably clever, actually bears a strong resemblance to the sign of Cancer. The Jackdaw is attracted by bright, pretty objects, especially those which gleam in the sun. He will litter his nest with milk-bottle tops, diamond rings, or silver coins, then sit upon his hoard gleefully – just like a dragon upon its pile of gold. A Cancerian is a collector too. It won't matter if your collection is valuable or not. If it is pretty, or suits your taste, or (even better) having sentimental value – you will treasure it forever.

KITCHEN – Many of the world's finest chefs are Cancerian. This love of *haute cuisine* perfectly combines the true talents of creativity, imagination, and the desire to nurture others. Of course you don't all reach such heights of grandeur – but most Cancerians are fairly domesticated, and also quite 'at home' pottering about in the kitchen.

LATERAL THINKING – Just as the crab is renowned for side-stepping, the Cancerian is rather good at finding alternative ways around obstacles or to solve problems. This will not necessarily be the longest way round either – it may be a way that no-one else has thought of. For this reason, many Cancerians are good at cryptic puzzles or crosswords, or at simply evolving different methods to achieve traditional results.

MEMORY – Said to have the longest memory in the Zodiac – especially the long-term kind, many Cancerians can remember events which happened in their toddling days. The Moon (ruler of Cancer) is also strongly associated with racial memory, so experiences of *Déjà vu* are fairly common with this sign.

NAÏVE – This can be a great disadvantage to some Cancerians as (trusting souls), they tend to take others at face value and believe everything they are told. This is because they find it difficult to imagine that everyone else is not as humane and caring as they are. So take care – you could be an 'innocent abroad'.

OVERSENSITIVE – Another Cancerian disadvantage. You may quickly rise to the bait or overreact if you think someone is criticising you and yours, or getting at you. In fact, this could be just a humorous jibe or dig which most people tolerate in their daily lives. You should become more thick-skinned with experience.

PEARL – Jewel of the ocean. The most well-known precious stone associated with Cancer. Others are: mother-of-pearl (nacre), abalone shell, moonstone, agate, or rose quartz (if a June birthday). You should try to own jewellery, cufflinks, ornaments, etc. which contain at least some of these affinitive stones – especially pearl.

QUIET – A rumour about the sign of Cancer which is not necessarily true – it will depend upon many other factors in your horoscope. But generally speaking, Cancer is a listener rather than an informer, so even if you do chat, you can probably do so without giving anything much away.

RETICENT – Many Cancerians lack confidence, which is rather a shame for such a resourceful and imaginative sign. Yet you may be quite backward about coming forward and may shun the limelight. You must try to remember that you are just as good as anyone else, although you might feel different. Everyone is unique and different, even though most prefer to run with the herd.

SILVER – This is the precious metal most strongly associated with the moon and therefore with the sign of Cancer. It symbolises purity – hence its use at weddings and christenings, and is noted to be a strong defence against the forces of evil, as in silver bullets for vampires, etc. Silver is also traditionally used in the photographic trade – a Cancerian favourite.

TENACIOUS – In extreme cases, this can become a major fault. The 'clinging' quality of Cancer can produce the mother who cannot let her child go, and follows him/her into marriage, causing friction between herself and the partner, OR the over-possessive husband, who becomes quite chauvinistic towards his wife – never letting her out of his sight.

The more positive results of this trait are shown in those who have large families, become foster parents, teachers, nurses, doctors, or carers – because these have to spread their concern in a thinner fashion.

UNWORLDLY – Yes, this is the most unworldly of signs, apart from Pisces. You may often be considered to be away with the fairies or on another planet. Do not let this bother you unduly. You can be quite realistic when the need arises, for you live in the best of both worlds.

VALIANT – Contrary to popular belief, it takes far more courage to forge ahead with something that you secretly fear, than it does to boldly go forth and tackle that which comes easily, though much acclaimed by others. This former action is true bravery indeed.

WHITE – The true colour of Cancer. Other associated colours are grey, silver-grey, or dark green. 'White' may also refer to food colour. You may enjoy white creamy foods, such as, mashed potatoes, fish in parsley sauce, ice-cream, milk puddings, etc.

XANADU – A place of dreamlike magnificence and luxury – probably every Cancerian's dream of Heaven.

YEW – A coniferous tree strongly associated with the sign of Cancer. Often planted in churchyards to represent remembrance and sympathy.
In the past, this wood was traditionally favoured for the making of bows, due to its strength and yielding qualities: both Cancerian attributes.

ZODIAC – The twelve major constellations which surround our solar system, though there are many others. The sign of Cancer may be particularly adept at recognising or reading these, or may simply be intrigued by them.

Where there's a will there's a way

LEO

Leo

Leo is the King of signs
He'll always run the show
But don't you steal his thunder
Simply bask within his glow

ABC of Leo

ATTRACTIVE – Though Leo is often majestic in looks, this description rather refers to personality. You are definitely the magnetic type. People will buzz around you like bees around a honey pot. Provided your sun is well-aspected, your popularity is assured.

BOSSY – You can be. As a natural-born leader, sometimes it is difficult for you to tolerate slower-minded individuals. You might feel that these types could do with a swift butt-kick. And, of course, this is what gives you your managerial potential.

COURAGEOUS – Yes, you are brave as a lion, though you don't really need to be, as confidence is your middle name. You should have no qualms about taking centre stage – any time.

DRAMATIC – Leo's often make good actors or actresses, because in this way, they can truly express what they feel, without any fear of reprisal from alien types. You can also be quite melodramatic in your personal life. Beware of flooring the more down-to-earth types.

EGOCENTRIC – You are the centre of the Universe, as far as you are concerned. But this is not meant as selfishness or self-seeking on your part, for Leo is the most generous of signs. You require only recognition and appreciation of your grandiose efforts. Upon these things you will thrive and become even better.

FIRE – As the fixed fire sign, you are sure to burn the brightest. Your progressive and creative instincts are incredibly strong, and have been since your earliest days. The danger here is that because success and achievement come to you so easily, you may become a bit lazy, and inclined to rest upon your laurels, so to speak. This could bring dissatisfaction with yourself in the long run; it would not be good for your Leonian pride.

GOLD – The precious metal most associated with Leo. It symbolises richness and truth. In its raw state: gold bullion, it is the mainstay of most national wealth and currency. Also much used in the making of jewellery and other precious items, as it is both malleable and untarnishable.
   Gold, as a colour, as well as associated shades of orange, yellow, apricot, etc. are all eminently suitable for Leo.

HEART – This is the body part which is most associated with Leo. Very aptly, as Leo is at the heart of the Zodiac, ruled by the sun which is the heart of the solar system. You may need to take very great care of this vital organ; either that or it will be the strongest and healthiest part of you. Many sayings and phrases have been coined concerning the heart: e.g. 'big-hearted', 'hearty appetite' or 'heartfelt thanks'.
   Any of these could easily apply to Leo.

IMPERIAL – No other sign has such an air of majesty and regality, quite unconsciously. It will show in the way that you walk, the way that you hold yourself – very erect, and even in the way you can flare your nostrils.

A Leo seems to have a built-in knack of looking down upon others – even taller people. Most of you are probably descended from ancient kings and queens, so there should be a tinge of royalty in your blood.

JOVIAL – Jocular, happy, cheerful, in good spirits, merry, mirthful, blithe, buoyant, animated, convivial, sociable, cordial. You can be the 'life and soul' of any party.

KIND – You love your fellow man in the sense that you long to help and guide him or her. You would make a very good teacher or master of arts for this same reason.

You can be generous to a fault. All you ask in return is recognition and respect.

LOVEABLE – It's almost impossible to dislike a Leo. It seems that Nature has endowed you with this sunny and loveable disposition as a special gift to enhance your leadership qualities. People will follow you because they like you – not because they feel subdued. That in itself is your power.

MANE – A fine head of thick hair: the lion's mane, should be naturally yours, particularly in youth. This hair is often blond or having a reddish tinge. It is the same for males and females alike. Even if you are not naturally blond, you may be tempted at some stage to add highlights or reddish lowlights. The hair often recedes from the forehead in males, but whatever is left will still be thick and abundant. In females, the hair should remain a crowning glory throughout life.

NOBLE – Your moral qualities are commendable and your ideals are high. You should have great character, being honorable, admirable and free from any pettiness or meanness. Some chauvinistic or feminist tendencies could develop, however, neither of which would go down well in today's society.

OVERT – There is nothing secretive about you. You are fully prepared to share your knowledge with the world, or even publicise if necessary. You would make a good public speaker, an honest politician, or even a president.

PROUD – This essential Leonian pride is not limited to the self, although self-respect is crucial. It also extends to partners, children, friends and associates. For example: you would be quite mortified if a partner dressed carelessly or misbehaved in public; or you would be quite upset if your child failed all his school exams.

　　These things are unlikely to happen to a Leo, because those close to you naturally want to please and to bask in your reflected glory.

QUARTZ – This clear basic crystal: the stuff of which crystal balls are made, is believed to be good for the brain and soul by dispelling negativity. It is said to store information and aid dream recall. It would be a good one for Leo to own, as you despise negativity in any form.

RUBY – A variety of corundum. This is the precious stone which is most associated with Leo. Richly red, you can almost feel its inner fire. It is reputed to boost the immune system. You should try to own at least one of these fiery gems.

SUN – The ruler of Leo. This represents your ego, creativity, and self-expression, and is what gives you your natural sunny disposition. As a Leo, you were born to 'shine'. Just be sure that you do.

TASTEFUL – Yes, your good taste is commendable, whether it be for food, fashion, décor, cars, or venues. You don't care for anything cheap or tacky.

Never forget that taste is based upon personal preference – not everyone's is the same as yours.

UNRELENTING – As the fixed fire sign, you will not be deterred from your chosen path by anyone or anything. This is what makes you such a positive leader. However, you might find it helpful and enlightening to listen to some other points of view sometimes.

VAIN – The Leonian child will spend much time gazing into mirrors, as soon as he/she is old enough to know what mirrors are for. True – the desire for beauty comes from the sun ruler which demands that you shine. But parents need to instil into the child that true beauty comes from within – the beautiful person will be loved far more than the beautiful face.

WORTHY – A Leo is distinguished by good qualities, usually deserving of honour or respect. Leo is morally upright, and probably could not bear to be scandalised or cheapened in any way. This modern trend about the Paparazzi hunting down the Royals, and reporting their personal lives for the sake of a few bucks, is probably most distasteful to you.

XERXES – *c.*519-465 BC, son of Darius I, king of Persia 486-465. When his father died he inherited the task of taking revenge on the Greeks for their support of the Ionian cities that had revolted against Persian rule. His invasion force crossed the Hellespont with a bridge of boats, and in 480 won victories by sea at Artemisium and by land at Thermopylae. There was a king indeed.

YEATS – William Butler (1865-1939). An Irish poet and dramatist. In his poetry, the elaborate style of his earlier work was influenced by the Pre-Raphaelites. Yeats served as a senator of the Irish Free State (1922-8) and was awarded the Nobel Prize for literature in 1923. Although a Gemini, he definitely led a Leonian life.

ZENITH – The highest or culminating point in power, prosperity, etc. You, as a Leo, should work towards this – it being your ultimate and greatest goal.

All that glitters...

VIRGO

Virgo

Virgo is particular
She'll wear a worried frown
While she straightens up your tie
And dusts your shoulders down

ABC of Virgo

ANTAGONISM – This is a sign which worries a lot, often without due cause. You may be hard-working, industrious and faithful, but may sometimes lose sight of the overall task with your insistence upon fine detail and perfection.

Always take care that you do not lose sight of the wood while you are studying the trees.

BREAD – Virgo is a very basic sign, and bread is a very basic food. You may therefore find this included in most of your meals, whether or not you are a vegetarian. 'Bread' as a colloquial term, also implies 'living' and 'earning' – both very basic Virgoan considerations.

CUPID'S BOW – The mouth of a Virgo is the most perfectly-formed and mobile of features. Usually small and neat, but very flexible, often with a pronounced cupid's bow. You will use this mouth extensively – perhaps even excessively. You should therefore be a great talker, whistler, taster, kisser, or simply have the most expressive of features.

DISCRIMINATING – This sums Virgo up to a 'T'. You are particularly discerning about everything in your life, whether it be food, possessions, surroundings, or people – you definitely like to choose.

Be careful – there may be nothing much left that you actually like!

ECONOMICAL – Virgo does not tolerate waste, and is not inclined to overdo things. You are the 'happiest shopper' of all; you probably always write a list, and rigidly adhere to it, in spite of many temptations along the way. You may be exceptionally careful with money and possessions and anything you own will be cared for, appreciated and valued.

FINNICKY – Often nit-picky in childhood – you probably drove your parents mad with your likes and dislikes. Even now, you like your food to be nicely presented. You would not eat anything that looks horrible or unattractive.

Here's an idea for you: Sunshine Burger. Place large hamburger in centre of plate. Arrange chips (fries) radiating from burger to resemble rays. Use green peas for eyes and also for curly hair on top of head. Then sliced/chopped carrot for mouth and nose. Let your family eat with amusement.

GREEN – Ecologically sensitive? You should be, if you think about it, because you really care about the planet and what we, as a species, are doing to it. Maybe you don't drive a car, or if you do, you are sure to use unleaded petrol (gas). You could also be a keen cyclist, walker, or runner.

HYPER-ACTIVE – This applies to the most extreme Virgoan types. In childhood, you would have driven your parents to distraction with your abundant, buoyant energy. Even now, you just hate to be idle, and are never happier except when busy, busy, or even busier.

INDUSTRIOUS – Definitely the most hard-working of signs. You will work as hard for others as you do for yourself. You have terrific drive and enthusiasm for everything you do. Only take care not to wear yourself out.

JUST – Yes, you are honest and virtuous, and you believe in fairness and equality for all. Solomon is probably your patron saint. Remember the Bible story about the two women who claimed the same baby? Solomon said, 'Let the child be cut in half'. And to the woman who screamed, 'NO!' he gave the child.
   Your own wisdom and sense of justice should be as fine.

KIND-HEARTED – Of course you are naturally so. There probably isn't a cruel or aggressive bone in your body. As one of the most unselfish signs, you should remember to put your own interests first – at least some of the time.

LOYAL – Definitely the most faithful of signs – you will remain true throughout your life to all your friends, family members, partners, etc. even when this becomes most difficult.

MERCURY – The planet which rules Virgo (as well as Gemini). This is the planet of intellect and communication, so you should love to think as much as you love to talk. In mythology, Mercury (Hermes in Greek) was the messenger of the gods. With wings on his heels, he was noted for speed and reliability.

NEAT – You are quite naturally a neat person, and will suffer depression if you are in any way thwarted in your efforts to achieve this. You probably have files and folders for everything – so why not get on with all that organising that you love so well.

OVER-CONSCIENTIOUS – Again, this applies to extreme Virgoan types. Just because you are super-efficient, don't expect everyone else to be the same. Most of all – stop worrying! There are eleven other sign types in this world who manage quite well, without being absolutely perfect.

PRECISE – You probably have mathematical or scientific ability, or if you do not, your logical mind will express itself in various other perfectionist ways. Unpunctuality, scruffiness, or haphazard efforts from others, are things you do not tolerate well.

QUIZZICAL – You do not lack a sense of humour, though in this, as with everything else, you have your own standards of perfection.

RADIO – A great favourite with Virgo, along with the printed word. Because there is no visual aid to help the listener/reader, the dialogue has to be that much richer and more expressive.

SECRETARY – A Virgoan makes an excellent one, as bosses and managers are invariably disorganised, and Virgo's just love sorting others out. He/she will keep a perfect diary of appointments, arrange meetings, type up endless reports and letters, all tirelessly and efficiently.

TELE – You will enjoy conversing on the telephone, using CB radio, surfing the Internet, or sending e-mails, as these are all forms of telecommunication to which Virgo is well-suited. What on earth did Virgoans do before these things were invented? I expect they were the greatest diarists or letter-writers.

ULCERS – In extreme cases, Virgo is prone to worry and stress. So much so, that this could actually result in psychosomatic illness. Allowing yourself sufficient time for relaxation and pleasure should help a lot.

VERBOSE – Virgo is so in love with words that he/she may become a chatterbox, nag or gossip if not careful.
   In a more positive light, Virgoans make very good commentators, writers, poets, lecturers, or songwriters.

WALKING – You may be fond of the gentler 'earthy' sports, such as, rambling, cycling, caving, or watching ball games. Fine scenery will always appeal to you, so that all these outdoor activities should happen in idyllic places, wherever possible.

XANTHIPPE – (pronounced, zan-thippy). A fairly good example of the Virgoan potential. I expect you've heard of her. She was the wife of Socrates, proverbial as a shrew. History is not quite clear as to whether she drove him to greatness, or made his life hell. It was probably some of both.

YOUTHFUL – Virgo is reputed to keep youthful looks for longer than most. Ruled by Mercury, the young messenger of the gods, this is not surprising. Often thin and wiry in youth, this sign tends to gain weight fairly fast, but even then, it is often of the chubby, cherubic kind, and is not unappealing.

ZOOLOGY – Virgo seems to have a natural affinity with animals and may be quite knowledgeable about certain species. Animals often replace people or children in the affection of Virgoans. Even if you are far too busy to keep a pet of your own, you will probably keep pictures, stories, films, or models of your favourites.

"Blessed are the meek, for they shall inherit the earth"

LIBRA

Libra

Libra's quite the charming type
With the world's most winning smile
He'll get away with murder
With his easy-going style

ABC of LIBRA

AMIABLE – Certainly the friendliest of signs – the most sociable, amenable, and gregarious. Libra *loves* people. And people cannot help loving Librans in return, simply because they are so loveable.

BENEVOLENT – Kind, considerate and generous, you can always be relied upon to give to a worthy cause. You also have no qualms about treating your friends, though you might not always remember their birthdays, even though they always remember yours.

CHARMING – As the most pleasant and attractive of signs, Libra naturally possesses all the social graces. The Libran smile is reputed to melt the hardest heart, and often comes complete with dimples. You could probably charm the birds off the trees or get away with murder; but take care not to overdo it, else you could acquire a reputation for insincerity or fickleness.

DISORIENTATED – Probably the most muddle-headed of all signs, apart from Pisces. You will lose things, forget things, or remember things wrongly.

As you are the Cardinal air sign, you are probably more 'up in the air' than most people, and rarely have your feet down on earth.

ELEGANT – Libran taste and sense of style are hard to beat. You always manage to look just right whatever the occasion. And, as you are quite artistic, this will show in your choices of dress, furniture, décor, food, etc.

Fashion, beauty, art or design are often career considerations for Libra.

FAIR – Essentially fair and unbiased, you believe in equal shares for all, and cannot come to terms with injustice of any kind.

'It's not fair!' was probably your favourite cry as a child. Quite possibly it still is.

GREGARIOUS – As a very sociable animal, you will spend much of your spare time with friends or colleagues at parties, clubs and social events. You enjoy 'living it up' and indeed, living life to the fullest. You are also a good 'team-player' and work well within partnerships.

Loneliness of any kind is hard for a Libran to bear.

HARMONIOUS – Harmony is your pet word and, for you, 'Love makes the world go round'. You dislike quarrels or upset of any kind which may rock the smooth sailing of your little boat. That old Hippie adage, 'Make love, not War' would have been just perfect for you.

INDECISIVE – This is a Libran disadvantage. You will always seek the advice of another, often of several others, before making any major decision then, after an age of wavering, will finally go ahead and do what you first thought of doing. Yet you really need these opinions from others, just to weigh up the 'pro's and cons' and to make sure that your final decision is the right one.

JUST – Although non-judgemental by nature, you absolutely hate injustice and will do your best to oppose it, especially if this is directed towards your friends or colleagues. You would definitely make a good lawyer and, like a knight of old, you could become a Champion of Justice.

KIDNEYS – The body part most associated with Libra. You can take best care of these by drinking lots of pure water and avoiding excessive sugar intake or alcohol. This can sometimes be quite difficult for a Libran who enjoys luxury foods of all kinds.

LUXURY – Ruled by the planet Venus, you are innately fond of the good life. The best and finest of everything will tempt you, whether it be food, drink, fine clothes, possessions, or surroundings – you will find second-best difficult to accept.

MIRTH – Naturally a happy soul, you are almost always smiling, and like nothing better than a good laugh. You will enjoy sharing jokes with friends, either verbal or practical, and some of your humour can be quite ribald, which can be surprising for such a genteel person!

NONCHALANT – Calm and casual, lacking in enthusiasm or interest, indifferent, unconcerned. This is a pose you may adopt, especially within your social environment. Yet it is far from the truth. You care quite a lot about your special friends; you just find it difficult to concentrate upon any one at a time, simply because they are so many.

However, this trait will make you the perfect party host, as you are so good at mingling.

OPULENT – If you were not born rich and affluent, then you will spend your life trying to become so. A poor Libran is a discontented one, but never mind – you can easily charm your way to the top of the ladder.

PEACEABLE – Yes, you are the original peacemaker: the mediator. As you find aggression so distasteful, you will go out of your way to become a go-between for your warring friends, although you will find it impossible to take sides.

QUAINT – In the true sense of 'attractively unusual', 'pleasantly charming' and sweet, you most certainly are. If you were a painting, you would certainly be of the 'chocolate box' variety.

RHYTHM – This comes easily to you, whether it be in dancing, singing, or writing poetry, you seem to have a built-in metronome. For you, there will never be a step, note, or word out of synch.

SAPPHIRE – The precious stone most strongly associated with Libra. Dark blue in colour – some of the highest quality gems are almost black. It is symbolic of peace and tranquillity.

THOUGHTFUL – Yes, you naturally are, when you remember to be. You are kind and considerate to all of your friends and colleagues. You will take cakes and sweets into work, even when it isn't your birthday. Let's hope they all appreciate you in return.

UNRELIABLE – Unfortunately, Librans often are. This is not because they mean to be – quite to the contrary. A Libran has so many friends and dates in their diary – that's if they remember to keep one – that they simply cannot keep up with them all, and therefore cannot help but let down a few. The Libran memory is not so hot anyway.

VENUS – The planet which rules Libra, along with Taurus. This is the planet of love, luxury and indulgence. Often seen at this (Libran) time of year, as a bright shining star, just after sundown, and before any real stars are visible: The Evening Star.

WELL-BALANCED – You should be, for the scales are your astrological symbol. A Libran hates imbalance or disharmony of any kind, so you probably like to keep things on an even keel.
　　You like equality too – especially between the sexes. You will never a Chauvinist nor a Feminist be.

X – Meaning 'kiss'. This character is sure to appear at the end of all Libra's personal communications – family letters, invitations, notes to friends, e-mails and, of course, love letters. Libra should be particularly good at the latter.

YUM – This is how you feel about food and drink. You enjoy the finest and best. You like it to be attractively presented, and could become quite a connoisseur or a gourmand. You could also become a chocoholic or a wine-glugger. Always remember to watch your weight.

ZABAGLIONE – A dessert consisting of egg-yolks, sugar, and (usually Marsala) wine, whipped to a frothy texture over a gentle heat and served either hot or cold. A perfect choice for Libra.

Handsome is as handsome does

SCORPIO

Scorpio

Scorpio's a 'femme fatale'
Alluring, deep and haunting
But if you rouse her jealous streak
Her vengeance will be daunting

ABC of SCORPIO

ALLURING – Scorpio possesses great charm in an indefinable kind of way which is really best described as sexual magnetism. So, you could either be a 'femme fatale' or a 'Lothario'.

BURGUNDY – As a colour (dark red), burgundy is associated with Mars which was the old ruler of Scorpio, before the discovery of Pluto.
This is also the colour of bloodstone, a traditional jewel of this sign. And, as a drink, Burgundy, a rich dark wine, named for its place of origin, should also be pleasing to Scorpio.

CHRYSANTHEMUM – A member of the daisy family, with long powerful roots. This attractive late-flowering plant comes in many colours, and brightens many gardens, in the northern hemisphere, from September to late November.

DETECTIVE – Scorpio likes to get to the roots and sources of things and will gain great satisfaction from seeking the truth. Research of any kind will therefore be painstaking and thorough.
Police work or scientific research are often good career choices for Scorpio.

EXTREME – Definitely not a 'middle of the road' sign. You may veer from one extreme to the other. Like that little child in the old nursery rhyme, 'When you are good, you are very, very good, but when you are bad you are horrid.' There is no sitting on the fence for you!

FAITHFUL – Yes, you are the most loyal and faithful of signs, probably even more so than your affinitive sign: Cancer. Once you have fallen in love, it will be forever, and you may find rejection extremely difficult to accept.
   Take care not to become obsessive.

GENIUS – Quite often true of Scorpio, though the name literally means 'born to begin' (as in generic). So deep are your thought processes and your desire to unearth roots, that you are almost bound to turn up something new and wonderful now and again.

HIGHLY-SEXED – Probably having the highest libido in the Zodiac, you were simply designed to procreate. You are definitely not 'nun' or 'monk' material. Even those of you who don't want children will still have enormous fun doing the necessary. The celibate life is definitely not on your agenda.

INTENSE – You don't believe in doing anything by halves. You will either do it exceptionally well – even over the top – or you won't bother doing it at all.

JEALOUS – This can be a major drawback for Scorpio, for you simply cannot stand competition or rivalry in any shape or form.
   The most positive outcome of this is: that you will always strive to be the best that you can be under any circumstances.

KRAKEN – A creature once believed to live in the very deepest ocean off the coast of Norway. It was said to 'awake' on very rare occasions in order to punish the wicked denizens of Earth, when its 'rise' would cause enormous tidal waves and mass destruction.

John Wyndham wrote *The Kraken Awakes*. Any Scorpio would probably love this book, and most of his others.

LEAD – The metal most strongly associated with Scorpio, due to its heaviness and solidity ('plumbus' in Latin). Lead was once widely-used in household plumbing, but has since become suspect for health reasons. It is still used as a protection against radiation, and also for plumb-bobs in building and in angling, to determine a direct vertical line to the ground, or river bed.

MYSTERIOUS – Deep and unfathomable, no-one ever truly understands a Scorpio – except perhaps another Scorpio (or a Cancer or Pisces). Even then, the differences are likely to be personal and unique, so that the 'understanding' is far from perfect. You probably don't even understand yourself, but not to worry – which you don't – your mysterious allure will always attract others like a magnet.

NETTLE – One of several plants associated with Scorpio due to its 'sting'. Scorpio is reputed to have 'a sting in the tail', that is, the sting will come when least expected. The nettle too, looks very soft and green, but when you try to gather it, tiny hairs on the leaf surface can give you a nasty itchy rash.

Nettle is still a valuable herb (gather with gloves). It is a rich source of iron, first brought to Britain by the Romans. Make nettle tea, soup or wine (refer to Merlin or Cadfael).

ONYX – A black shining stone, usually polished smooth and not faceted like other gems. Very reminiscent of the subtle cleverness of Scorpio.

PLUTO – The planet which rules Scorpio – the furthest known from the sun. Pluto is quite small – not much bigger than our own moon, yet it is incredibly dense and heavy – hence its association with lead.

In mythology, Pluto: Mephistopheles, was Lord of the Underworld, and of anything deep, dark and unknown.

QUAIL – Not to be confused with the OE expression for 'cringe' or 'flinch', this actually refers to a very amorous bird, known for its faithful and loveable habits.

In US slang, this word also refers to 'a tasty piece' of the opposite sex, a bit like 'crumpet' in UK.

And of course, quail eggs are quite a delicacy – eggs being 'sources' of this ardent bird.

REPRODUCTIVE SYSTEM – In both sexes, this set of body parts are most associated with Scorpio.

Be pleased to know that you are the sexiest sign of the Zodiac.

SECRETIVE – In your own right, you definitely are: sharing your innermost thoughts only with your nearest and dearest, if at all. But you are also the most trustworthy guardian of the secrets of others, probably the best confidant in the Zodiac.

You would make an excellent agony aunt or uncle (or a spy).

TACITURN – Yes, many Scorpio's are of the 'strong and silent' type rather than great conversationalists. This does not mean that you never speak to anyone; but generally a Scorpio speaks when he/she has something meaningful to say, and does not care for idle gossip or inane chatter. So any conversation with *you* is sure to be an interesting one, because it will concern something that you have thought about a great deal.

UNSHAKEABLE – Not entirely true, because you are deeply emotional; but you also have terrific control. You may therefore appear to be cool, unmoved, or deadpan, even when there is great turmoil going on within. Only take care that such rigid suppression does not cause you much inner stress and raise your blood pressure.

VENGEFUL – Although you are the most loyal and devoted friend imaginable, you do not dismiss betrayal lightly, and can also become the bitterest enemy. You can hold a grudge for the longest time, then may eventually soften and forgive – but you will never, ever forget.

WATCHFUL – You certainly don't miss much. You are the perfect 'shadow' or detective. You can so easily fade into the background while you listen and take note. The most observant of signs – you could probably research a whole novel without writing a single word in your notebook – your memory would suffice.

X-RAY – This rather exaggerated term is often used to describe Scorpian eyes. These may be deep, intense, penetrating, soul-searching, or simply magnetic, but are usually the most arresting feature.

Even your Scorpian child may have a noticeably fierce, intent gaze, that others will comment upon.

YAHOO – As everyone knows these days, this is an excellent 'search engine' (just like Scorpio). But the word originated in a tale by Jonathan Swift: *Gulliver's Travels*, which meant 'primitive man'. And, yes, a Scorpio is primitive in the best possible way, meaning 'basic'.

ZAP – Energy, power, vigour, drive, coupled with a strong emotional effect. This fairly sums up the word, as well as a Scorpio.

Still waters run deep

SAGITTARIUS

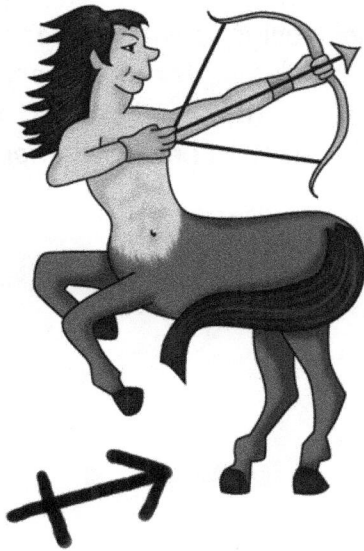

Sagittarius

Sagittarius is the restless one
With wanderlust galore
But if you stuff his head with books
He might remain on shore

ABC of SAGITTARIUS

ALERT – Sagittarius is the mutable (flexible) fire sign. You will always be ready and 'raring to go' for anything, and should never be caught napping. On your toes? You naturally are.

BLUNT – Like all fire signs, you are outspoken and honest. You can also be rather tactless sometimes. It's all too easy for you to open your mouth and put your foot in it – you probably do it every day. Diplomacy is not your best point.

CHANGEABLE – You are inclined to change your mind a lot, especially if your moon is in this same sign. However, you will pursue each change of heart just as vigorously as if it were your first choice.

DILIGENT – Yes, you are hardworking, in the sense that no effort is too much for you to achieve your desired goals. Yet you can also be side-tracked a lot. Try not to listen to people with new ideas. This may be difficult for you, at least until you have finished your current project.

ENTHUSIASTIC – Few signs are as enthusiastic as you. With jolly Jupiter as your ruler, you will bound and bounce your way through every new project. You also have the knack of firing others with your own eagerness. People will look to you for inspiration. As a natural crowd-puller, your popularity is assured. Just be sure that you can promise what you preach.

FREEDOM – This is the sign of freedom and restlessness. You just hate to be tied down or restricted in any form or fashion. In youth, this could cause a few problems. There will be those who suspect your ability to hold down a job. However, once your full potential is realised, you may find that you are actually 'head-hunted' or sought after. Don't forget that employers tend to do this on the cheap – they just enjoy grabbing valuable people, then stifling them. Self-employment or working freelance would be ideal for you.

GENEROUS – You don't just enjoy giving to others – you simply love throwing your money around. You are the original 'Big Spender', buying drinks for everyone in the room, perhaps without any thought for what you will get in return. And you don't do things like this just to 'buy' friendship – you don't need to, as friends are yours in abundance. You do it simply because you love people.

HIPS – Along with the lower back and thighs, these are the body parts most strongly associated with Sagittarius. Yours could be weighty and powerful. If you are a lady, no amount of dieting will ever reduce them. Nature has obviously intended you to be a great runner, cyclist, walker, climber or dancer. Be sure to use your talents well.

INCONSISTENT – You tend to spread your energies in as many directions as possible, only because you have such natural exuberance about everything. However, it is humanly impossible to keep up maximum enthusiasm for all things at all times, so, from some points of view, you may seem to flag, wane, or forget all about them. The Sagittarian memory is short in any case.

JUPITER – Your ruling planet (known as Zeus in Ancient Greek). This is the largest planet in our solar system, and therefore represents everything large, expansive or magnificent. So even if you are not terribly tall (depending on the position of Jupiter in your Natal Chart), you may still have to watch your weight – always.

KNOWLEDGEABLE – A Sagittarian craves knowledge in the same way that a smoker craves a cigarette, or an alcoholic craves a drink. Your desire to learn is insurmountable. University (or college) is an absolute 'must' for you (or your Sagittarian child). Your ideals are of the highest calibre, and your ambitions the greatest.
    You really do need to know it all.

LAW-ABIDING – A dishonest Sagittarian is rare. This would really go against the grain. Even if you did join a 'den of thieves' so to speak, you would probably be the first one to own up or 'let the cat out of the bag'. You will definitely feel more comfortable being honest and true to yourself. Always use your conscience as a guide.

MOODY – You may experience wide mood swings, from euphoric to deepest depression, and these may occur with alarming suddenness, leaving your friends and loved ones totally mystified. Tell them, and rest assured yourself, these 'down-swings' will not last long – the next day, you will have bounced right up again.

NON-CONFORMIST – Although honest, law-abiding and just, you may not always agree with 'the powers that be'. You will openly voice your opinions, should this be the case, and will probably gain many followers. You could easily form your own political party.

OPTIMISTIC – *Always to look on the bright side* is your legacy from the stars. No matter what happens in your life, you are never a defeatist, whatever setbacks may occur to thwart you. Hope is always on the horizon, and you will continually work towards this 'greener grass over the hill' concept.

PURPLE – This is the colour most strongly associated with Sagittarius. It has nothing to do with mourning, doom and gloom, as advocated by the Christian Church in Lent. Also, it has nothing to do with homosexuality, or its associations in USA. Purple is a beautiful colour, reminiscent of violet – the final colour of the spectrum, just before it turns red again.

Purple is an equal mixture of red and blue, that is, energy and wisdom. You should wear it with pride.

QUICK-WITTED – Along with Gemini (your opposite Sign), you are the master of 'quick repartit' and the eternal joker. You can always be relied upon to add a quip or funny comment to any conversation, which will make people laugh. You have the rare ability to lighten up any situation, no matter how dire. Even when you are on your deathbed, you will probably tell a 'passing' joke.

RESTLESS – A Sagittarian can hardly bear to keep still for a moment. You will find yourself falling asleep during lectures, or at the cinema, much to the consternation of friends and companions. This does not mean that you are uninterested – but you simply cannot learn this way. For you, more than for any other sign, 'Learning is Doing'.

SPORTY – Many Sagittarians are athletic, having powerful legs, hips and thighs. Lots of you may be marathon runners, dancers, cyclists, or footballers. Tina Turner is a classic (physical) example of Sagittarius – just look at those hips and thighs...

TOPAZ – The precious stone most strongly associated with Sagittarius. The pale blue kind is most commonly used for jewellery; but there is also a 'golden' (orange-yellow) kind, which you would do well to seek out.
   Topaz represents richness, wisdom and glory.

UNPREDICTABLE – Unfortunately, you *can* be. Because of your inclination to 'go off at a tangent', or to enthuse about every new idea, people may not know quite what to expect next of you. They will wait with bated breath, and will probably not be disappointed.

VARIABLE – Changeable, mutable, chameleonic, protean, shifting, fluctuating, wavering, vacillating, inconstant, unsteady, unstable, fitful, capricious, fickle, blowing hot and cold. You could become all or any of these. Take care...

WILD FLOWERS – Most strongly associated with Sagittarius, these little heroes can grow anywhere in the most awful conditions. Once freely picked by children to take home, these days they are protected and barred from public picking. It's rather a shame really, because most people would dig up the root and transplant them into their own gardens, thereby preserving the species. Bluebells, primroses, foxgloves, cowslips – these are just a few facing extinction.

X - Xavier, St Francis (known as the 'Apostle of the Indies') [1506-52], Spanish missionary. He was ordained in 1537, and from 1540 onwards made a series of missionary journeys to southern India, Malacca, the Moluccas, Sri Lanka, and Japan, during which he made many thousands of converts. He died while on his way to China. Feast day, 3rd December. Whether you agree with his motives or not, he was definitely a Sagittarian.

YEARNING – This fairly sums up the Sagittarian life: the longing to grow and expand – the supposedly unreachable ideals which are yours to master. If you don't believe me, why not get on and do it? You might surprise yourself.

ZANY – Eccentric, peculiar, odd, absurd, comic, clownish, madcap, funny, amusing. These can also be Sagittarian attributes. If these are yours, why not use them to your advantage?

A rolling stone gathers no moss

CAPRICORN

Capricorn

Capricorn's a cautious type
Who bides her time with care
She'll reach the top eventually
With grey streaks in her hair

ABC of CAPRICORN

AMBITIOUS – Capricorn is the sign of prudence and ambition. You will bide your time, and know instinctively the exact right moment to push yourself forward. You are certainly ambitious, but never at the cost of security. That's why you will wait until you are absolutely ready.

BONES – Along with teeth and nails, these are the body parts most associated with Capricorn. Many of you may have good bone structure and therefore be quite photogenic. Your bones will need lifelong care, however, if they are not to become brittle in later life. Hopefully, you will drink lots of milk, or some other calcium intake, so that yours will be just fine.

CAUTIOUS – No other sign is more careful than you. You don't believe in diving in head first and taking your chances. For you, scouting and exploring any given situation is vital. You probably wouldn't even consider marrying anyone unless you had thoroughly researched their life history.

DILIGENT – You are certainly not afraid of hard work, especially if you are self-employed. Being thorough and methodical, 'slow but sure' is your usual policy

ECONOMICAL – This does not necessarily mean that you are a Scrooge; but you are probably careful and wise with your money. Most likely you always check your till receipts. And, unlike less careful souls, you always consider the 'pros and cons' before you spend.

FEAR – This doesn't mean that Capricorns are fraidy-cats! But every sign has some special fear, even if they won't admit to it. Hopefully, yours won't be heights, because that is where you are headed.
  Your worst fear is probably of failure, though with all your hard work and determination, this seems very unlikely to occur.

GARNET – The precious stone most strongly associated with Capricorn. Dark red in colour, it is said to be therapeutic in times of trauma, and should always be worn close to the skin.

HUMOUR – Capricornian humour is usually of the dry and laconic variety. You can keep the straightest face while telling a joke, and your snippets of wit and sarcasm should be delivered with perfect timing.

INDEPENDENT – Self-sufficient, regardless of your status, you do not like to be beholden to anyone. You also dislike being in debt and will therefore work very hard to remain solvent.

JUDGEMENT – Yours is pretty cool and shrewd. You don't allow your heart to rule your head, and you are not very tolerant towards empty-headed or shallow types.

KEEN – This mostly applies to your sense of values, which are quite exceptional. You can easily judge the weight or distance of something with a mere glance. You have this kind of natural astuteness.

LOGICAL – Capricorn is the most logical sign, having a clear-cut, concise way of thinking. Many of you may have mathematical or scientific leanings, and probably like the most difficult crossword puzzles.

MEMORY – Yours is probably the best in the world, seconded only by your opposite sign: Cancer. You can probably remember things which happened when you were a tiny tot, as well as everything you learned at school. This, of course, will be very useful to you in passing exams, and you should also excel at trivia games and quizzes.

NAILS – Along with bones and teeth, these body parts are relevant to Capricorn. You will try to keep them neatly manicured, though if you type or do manual work, or gardening, this is not always easy.
  Calcium is said to strengthen nails, as well as gelatine.

OLIVE – A dark green fruit, sometimes black, strongly associated with Capricorn. It is particularly tasty in salads or on pizzas. The oil it gives, though expensive, is well worth adding to your shopping list in place of ordinary vegetable oil.
  Olive green, as a colour, always looks smart and often suits Capricornian types.

PRUDENT – This is one of the keywords for Capricorn. You take care in following the most politic and profitable course; showing sound judgement in practical affairs; circumspect, sensible and canny. That's you all over.

QUALITY – This will always be more important to you than quantity. For example: your wardrobe may contain few designer clothes, and even less 'down the market' ones. Your designer clothes will be carefully preserved and looked after. Apart from those essential business suits, they will most likely comprise classic suits or ball gowns which can be called to order for any important occasion.

RESERVED – Although not really shy, a Capricorn likes to preserve his/her reputation, and is therefore quite gentlemanly or ladylike in the public eye. For this reason, it could be unthinkable for you to 'let your hair down' or misbehave, and you would be quite mortified if a friend or partner did so.

Sometimes you might consider lightening up just a teeny-weeny bit.

SATURN – This is the planet which rules Capricorn. As a very slow-moving body, it is traditionally thought to represent delay and frustration. Personified in literature as 'Old Father Time'.

These days, Saturn is known to bring the unique kind of wisdom that comes only from experience.

TEETH – Along with bones and nails, these are the body parts most associated with Capricorn. In fact, dentistry is quite a popular career choice for this sign. Your teeth should either be exceptionally strong and healthy, or will need special care and attention. Whichever is the case, don't neglect your dentist, or else become one.

UNRELENTING – You are the Cardinal (leading) earth sign. Your birth heralds the approach of winter in most of our northern climes. There is no way that you can go back or reconsider anything. 'What's done is done' in your book.

VEGETARIAN – Of course, not all Capricorns are veggies, but this is one of the most likely signs to give it a try. You tend to prefer plain food in any case rather than 'concoctions', as you like to recognise what you are eating.

Veganism, however, would not be a good idea for you, as you really need the calcium contained in milk, cheese and eggs.

WISE – With Saturn as your ruling planet, you most definitely are. Even in childhood, you would have had an 'old head upon young shoulders' and astounded people with your wisdom.

Don't forget that 'all work and no play makes Jack a dull boy'.

X – As a Roman numeral, equates to ten, and Capricorn is the 10th Zodiac sign. What could be plainer and more Capricornian?

YARROW – A plant which grows in dry conditions, having feathery leaves and tiny composite flowers of white or pink, much favoured for making herbal tea, etc. Don't crush and kill if you find it growing in your lawn. This is an excellent herbal tonic. Pick it by all means, then dry it, freeze it, preserve it until the next time you need a quick 'pick-me-up'. You could be delighted.

ZENITH – The highest point of the heavens, or the highest point of the sun, as at noon. The Midheaven in Astrology. Again most appropriate for Capricorn.

As the 10th Sign, you are right up there at the top of the Chart Wheel. Up is the only way you will ever want to go.

From little acorns mighty oak trees grow

AQUARIUS

Aquarius

Aquarius is different
From anyone you know
With wilful independence
He will his own way go

ABC of AQUARIUS

AMETHYST – The precious stone most strongly associated with Aquarius, varying in colour from pale lilac to deepest purple. Said to be a powerful aid to creative thinking, spiritual awareness and healing. Also believed to combat insomnia and to protect from the harmful effects of alcohol.
   Every Aquarian should own one.

BLUE – The ideal colour for Aquarius. Of course there are many shades of this colour, but sky blue seems the most suitable choice, as your ruling planet, Uranus was once 'god of the sky'.

CIRCULATION – Along with the knees and lower legs, this is the body part most associated with Aquarius. You probably always have cool hands and feet and, in extreme cases, these can literally turn blue with the cold. You really need to keep these parts warm and should always wear gloves and boots in winter.

DETACHED – You can seem to be detached, even aloof; but this is usually when your mind is off 'on another planet'. Close friends or partners will understand this very well, and might occasionally knock on your head and ask if anyone's in.

ECCENTRIC – Aquarius is often considered to be weird or at least 'a bit odd'. This is only because you have no desire to be one of the crowd or to 'run with the herd'. You are courageous enough to just be yourself. Most people will realise that you are a rare and wonderful person, once they've got over the initial shock.

FRIENDLY – Yes you are, especially within a social situation. You will want to meet and greet everyone at a party or large function. This can leave your nearest and dearest feeling somewhat neglected; but he or she will just have to get used to it, because this is the way that you are made.

GIFTED – Aquarius is often very talented. Your originality and inspiration are unequalled in the Zodiac. Many of you are inventors, writers, or will take up creative careers, because there is no-one else quite like you, or at least no-one who would do things the same way as you do.

HUMANITARIAN – Aquarians are very much so, in a very wide sense. You really care about all people, and the state of the earth as a planet, rather than concentrating upon individuals.

You would be the very one to sacrifice a few to save the many.

IMPERSONAL – Yours is probably the ideal voice to record on those automated message machines. Yes, Aquarius is emotionally on the cool side. Generally self-sufficient, you are well-liked and have no shortage of friends, yet you can take people or leave them. You can be equally happy chatting with friends in a bar, or curled up alone with a book. Lucky you. You can enjoy your own company and don't really need anyone else.

JUROR – You would make the perfect juror, because you can be totally unbiased and circumspective, without becoming emotionally influenced.

Obviously, juries have to be randomly selected, but it would be quite a good idea if they were all Aquarians.

KNEES – Along with the circulatory system and lower legs, these are the body parts most associated with Aquarius. If you are a lady, yours should be attractive and eye-catching. If you are a gent, they could be knobbly and muscular. In either case, they are sure to be noticed. Beware of rheumatic twinges as life goes on.

A cod-liver-oil supplement would be a good preventative measure.

LUCID – Clear and shining. This can refer to the Aquarian type of thinking or self-expression. It can also describe the eyes, which are often bright blue or green with a luminous quality.

MODERN – An Aquarian doesn't just like to keep up with the times, he/she is often way ahead of them. Yet although you love anything new and modern, you do not adhere blindly to the latest fashion – your taste and style are very much your own, so you could even be a trend-setter in your own right.

NURSE – A very good occupation for Aquarius, because your caring side can include everyone without you becoming emotionally involved with individuals. In an emergency, you will be the first on the scene with the fastest reactions. Thoroughly and efficiently, you could save lives with your 'no-nonsense' attitude.

OPINIONATED – Aquarian opinions are usually quite different from anyone else's – at the very least unorthodox, and sometimes quite outrageous. You have no qualms about airing your views and are very outspoken, even blunt.

But if a friend needs a truly honest opinion, they can always rely on yours.

PARADOX – You must be the original walking paradox, as you are friendly, yet aloof; sociable, yet liking your own company; highly technical, yet fanciful; caring, yet dispassionate.

Still you are luckier than most people, for you can view the world (and beyond) with wonder, and should never be bored in your life for a single moment.

QUIRKY – You have no shortage of unusual tastes or peculiarities. These could involve anything: food and drink, homes, cars, fashion, places to go, hobbies, or even weird friends.

For example: I know an Aquarian who adores cheese and marmalade sandwiches, another who won't drink from a coloured cup – it has to be white, and yet another who always pegs out socks on the washing-line, alternately one up-one down.

ROBUST – Aquarius is a fairly strong sign, being tough and resilient, with great resistance to most kinds of illness. Your only weakness seems to be 'cold'. This is something you don't tolerate well, and you may be inclined to succumb to colds, chills, and flu' as a result.

SPACE – Space-age; science-fiction; science-fantasy; astronomy; or astrology. These are subjects which often appeal to Aquarians – a weird mixture of reality and pseudo. But it is the futuristic theme that matters – that's what really grabs the imagination of this sign.

TANGENT – As an Aquarian, you are inclined to go off at one. This can be quite startling to your friends and family by its very suddenness, yet it should not be totally unexpected if they know you well. The trouble is, while you are exploring one situation, you can easily be intrigued by another, then that can lead to another, *ad infinitum*.

The only thing I can suggest is that you should make notes as you go.

URANUS – This is the heavenly body that rules Aquarius: the planet of eccentricity. It is so-called because of its unusual orbit. Uranus spins on its axis at a sharp angle of inclination, so that it is almost rotating on its back.

In mythology, Uranus was god of the sky and husband of Gaia (the Earth).

There is also Urania, the Greek Muse of Astronomy, usually depicted holding a globe. Hence these associations with the Sign of Aquarius.

VERNE Jules (1828-1905) – French novelist. Regarded as one of the first writers of science fiction. In his adventure stories, he often anticipated later scientific and technological developments. He explored the possibilities of space travel in *From the Earth to the Moon* (1865) and the use of submarines in *Twenty Thousand Leagues under the Sea* (1870). Other novels include *Journey to the Centre of the Earth* (1864) and *Around the World in Eighty Days* (1873). He was definitely far ahead of his time – most probably an Aquarius.

WILFUL – Definitely one of the strongest-willed signs, Aquarius will find it most difficult – nigh on impossible to surrender or accede to another, even for the noblest of reasons. In any battle of wills, discussion or compromise would probably work the best.

X-FILES – Sure to be a popular program with most Aquarians, as this explores all favourite subjects, such as: space; alien invasion; supernatural; and basically anything weird and wonderful.
    The stars (human ones) are nice too.

YEAR (Great) – 2000–4000 A.D marks the Age of Aquarius – the Great Year. **The Great Year** is the period of 25,868 years which the Solar System takes to pass through the influence of each of the twelve signs of the Zodiac. Each 'Great Month' lasts approximately 2,000 years. We have just emerged from the 'Great Year of Pisces' (Fishes = Christianity). Hopefully, the Age of Aquarius will bring in the 'Space Age' and great technological advancement which has already begun.

ZINC – A hard, lustrous, blueish-white metallic element which seems most suitable for Aquarius. As a mineral it's said to protect against colds and flu'. So might be well worth considering as a health supplement.

Love many, trust few ~ always paddle your own canoe

PISCES

Pisces

Pisces is a dreamer
Caring, sweet and kind
She'd really like to change the world
But can't make up her mind

ABC of PISCES

AQUAMARINE – The precious stone most suitable for Pisces. Its name literally means 'water of the sea' and it is a beautiful green-blue colour. This soothing gem is said to pacify nerves and banish phobias whilst ensuring tranquillity.

BROADMINDED – Pisces leaves no stone unturned in the consideration of 'Life, the Universe and Everything'*. To you, nothing is unbelievable until it has been disproved to your satisfaction (which is hardly ever). Therefore to God; UFO's; angels; fairies; ghosts; astrology; you give the benefit of the doubt – they are possibly all part of the same Great Mystery.
'The Truth is Out There'.

CREATIVE – One of the most creative signs in an artistic, rather than practical sense. Pisces is much associated with music, ballet, painting, poetry, acting, etc. This sign has an innate need for self-expression in some imaginative or beautiful form.

DOUBT – This refers to self-doubt rather than any lack of belief. Because Pisces is such an idealistic sign, you may seriously doubt your own ability to achieve your desired heights of perfection, and may often find yourself pulled in several possible directions anyway.
Unsure which path to follow? Why not try several during your life? You have both the ability and the inclination.

EUPHORIC – Pisces naturally seeks a state of emotional well-being, rapture, or bliss. Artistic expression and creative achievement can bring enormous satisfaction; but if this is neglected, or never quite attained to the desired standard, then the Piscean can take solace in over-eating; alcohol; smoking; or narcotic substances.

Some of our greatest artistic minds have succumbed to these influences in the past. Please don't let this happen to you.

FEET – The body part most associated with Pisces: the last and final sign of the Zodiac. Feet have to bear the weight (and often the brunt of abuse) of the rest of the body. They are often neglected or overworked. Who hasn't been 'rushed off their feet'? It is essential for a Piscean to take care of his/her feet, else problems are likely to occur. You should try to go barefoot as much as possible – and comfortable shoes are a *must*. As you know, if your feet hurt, you feel lousy all over, and the whole day is ruined.

Peppermint, lavender and rosemary are good soothing herbs to add to a foot bath.

GULLIBLE – Probably the world's most sympathetic and trusting sign (more so than its Cancerian affinity), Pisces finds it difficult to resist a sob story or disbelieve a promise. You should certainly steer clear of fast salespeople and always seek sound financial advice before taking on any large, expensive commitment. If you are an artist or a writer, you would be well-advised to get yourself an agent or an accountant.

HEART – Apart from soul, Pisces is almost all heart, and often allows this to rule the head. Probably the kindest and sincerest in the Zodiac, this sign would do practically anything to help anyone in need, without expecting anything in return. Genuinely loving and giving, you are probably also generous to charitable causes. The only thing which might contravene this remarkable trait is simple forgetfulness, for, being such a dreamer, Pisces is often distracted and absent-minded.

INTUITIVE – On a spiritual level, rather than a material one, there are many things which you just know to be true without knowing why. You will never quite trust this form of perception, however, and will always try to prove your hunches in other ways, yet you will often find that your first feeling was exactly right.

JACUZZI – As a water sign and the most restless of them, this could be the perfect form of relaxation for you after a hard day's work. You can even continue with your dreams and aspirations while you indulge. Warm jets of water soothing you all over... Neptune would have approved.

KALEIDOSCOPE – A bright array of constantly-changing pattern and colour. This is how the typical Piscean views his/her life. You have the ability to view the world with wonder in the same way that a child does, and you appreciate beauty and variety in all things. You just hate restriction, boredom, sameness or dullness.

LAZY – Pisces is often thought to be so, especially at school; when coping with housework; or judging by his/her cluttered work station. In actual fact, this sign is far from lazy in the subjects which fascinate him or her.

You have the ability to soak up knowledge like a sponge, if it is something you really want to know.

MALLEABLE – Especially in childhood, the Piscean can be shaped or moulded by parental or educational influence. When older, 'peer pressure' will add its effect. You will always want to be loved and accepted. This is fine, so long as you never allow your own talents and self-expression to take a back seat.

NEPTUNE – This is the planet which rules Pisces. It is a gaseous giant, 7th from the Sun, taking 156 years to complete its orbit, and staying in one sign for thirteen-fourteen years. Neptune is the Planet of vagueness and confusion – hence its association with Pisces. In mythology, Neptune was god of the sea (Poseidon in Greek). He was thought to cause squalls and tempests when upset, and woe betide ancient sailors who displeased him. Yet, this same god, when appeased, was also responsible for calm seas with a good following wind.

OTHERWORLDLY – Of or pertaining to an imaginary ideal or fantastic world. Quite the opposite of 'worldly'. It is difficult for a Pisces to be down-to-earth and realistic, no matter how much mundane knowledge is acquired. Some of you seem to exist in another realm completely, as if this one were the dream-state. But your imagination and creative ability are second to none.

PIXIE – The origin of this word is unknown, lost in the babble of ancient tongues. Yet, it is very reminiscent of Pisces and not by spelling alone. A Pixie is a type of Elf or Sprite (which any child could tell you), noted for its elusiveness, love of music, dance, and magic. The oldest recorded use of the word was in 'Pixie-Path' – a secret pathway, usually in woods, which caused humans to become lost and confused if they followed it.

QUESTING – As in all good tales of fantasy, sword 'n sorcery, chivalry, etc., a Piscean spends his/her life seeking, or working towards the Ideal.
Each of you has a metaphorical 'Holy Grail' to pursue.

RAINBOW – A natural phenomenon linked with Pisces due to its beauty and poetical association. An arc of concentric coloured bands (conventionally described as red, orange, yellow, green, blue, indigo, violet) seen in the sky in a direction opposite to the sun when its light reaches an observer after having been reflected and refracted by raindrops.
In Greek mythology, Iris was goddess of the Rainbow.

SPIRITUAL – Pisces is definitely more in tune with the soul (or psyche) than the body. In some cases, the body may become quite neglected, and you may need reminding to eat, exercise, groom, etc. Not every Pisces is religious; for some of you that would involve too much self-discipline. Many more of you are into philosophical subjects: astrology; mysticism; new age – anything which satisfies your need for fascination and awe.

THOUGHTFUL – In the sense of being considerate and sensitive to the needs of others – you definitely are. But in the literal sense, you are also likely to spend much of your time with your thoughts whirling. In this day and age when everything is so fast and hectic, it can be a serious disadvantage to be so preoccupied, and you may positively resent the fact that you 'don't get time to think'. You could try to set aside a period each day – perhaps when you are walking, jogging, or swimming: something which allows you to think at the same time. This would be excellent for sussing all those stories, poems, or designs which you might have in mind.

UNTIDY – It is difficult for a Pisces to be neat and tidy – that is definitely more of an earth consideration. There is often something unkempt about the appearance: fine unruly hair, for example; creases in clothing; or scuffs on your shoes – usually something you have forgotten, or cannot control. Around the house this trait is even worse. Have you ever walked into an artist's studio? Or a poet's kitchen? It's fairly true to say that the finest inspiration emerges from chaos.

VAGUE – One of Neptune's keywords; bestowed (in Neptune's case) due to its cloudy nature – impossible to discern the actual surface of the planet! A Piscean can also be indiscernible. This is usually caused by your tendency to distraction, which can flummox other people and make them think you are not quite 'with it'. You may also be absent-minded or forgetful, and may frequently miss appointments, or lose small possessions, such as, keys or pens. You could really do with keeping a diary, or a good secretary.

Overall, there is often an air of mystery surrounding this sign, which is not unattractive.

WINTER ACONITE – A suitable flower for Pisces. Sometimes known as Monkshood, this is one of the earliest plants to flower in northern climes. It seems to glow like a little golden flame from the hard earth. Though it is a virulent poison, Aconite has remarkable medicinal properties in the treatment of rheumatism and gout, to both of which Pisceans are prone.

X FACTOR – The first unknown or variable quantity in mathematics. Most Pisceans are invariably unknown (misunderstood) as well as infinitely variable.

YOGA – In Hindu philosophy, union of the self with the higher powers; a system of ascetic practice, meditation, etc. designed to achieve this. It would be a good practice for a Piscean, as it involves self-discipline combined with 'otherworldliness'.

ZEPHYR – Often (poetically) compared to Pisces: a mild and gentle breeze – usually a welcome one. The name is derived from Zephyrus, Greek god of the west wind, who brought forth the gentle rains of spring.

Every cloud has a silver lining

www.ingramcontent.com/pod-product-compliance
Lightning Source LLC
Chambersburg PA
CBHW060527030426
42337CB00015B/2003